Mindfulness

A Step-By-Step Beginners Guide on Living Your Everyday Life with Peace and Happiness by Becoming Stress Free

By

Isaiah Seber

©

2016

Table of Contents

Chapter 1: Introduction

"Wherever you are, be all there." – Jim Elliot

Are you tired? Are you stressed? Do you constantly find yourself filled with worry and anxiety? Are you consumed with everything you must get done, everything that is happening, and everything that has happened? Are you ready to make a change and start an adventure that will help you live in the present moment, stop your worries, and make your life more meaningful?

If you answered "yes" to any of these questions, then you are ready to take on a life of mindfulness. Give it a shot; read this book and try your hand at mindfulness for a few days. I promise you won't regret it. Whether you decide to totally transform your life to one of mindfulness and peace, or you simply want to add a few mindful moments into your day, you will see an improvement. Mindfulness has been proven as a stress reducer and life improver, take your shot now.

Take a minute to appreciate where you are. Think through your environment and your feelings. As you read through this mindfulness guide, attempt to focus fully on it. Start by examining your environment. What do you hear? Where are you sitting? How do you feel about where you are sitting? What people are near you? What else is on your mind? Consider all of these things, then re-focus your energy into this guide. As you read through the guide, try not to let your mind, focus, and attention wander. Ask yourself questions: How can I apply this? How does this make me feel? Is this for me? Keep yourself engages in this eBook and you will have done your first mindful task. When you reach the end, you will have successfully practiced mindfulness. If you did that, you can continue to do it.

Chapter 2: What is Mindfulness?

"Rule your mind or it will rule you." –

Buddha

Simply put, mindfulness is the practice of *living in the present moment.* Mindfulness is a change of lifestyle for the better. When you practice mindfulness, you practice existing in a non-judgmental state of awareness of the present moment. Mindfulness does not dwell on the past or the existence and issues that are beyond your control. Mindfulness means not worrying about the future and what will happen. Instead, when you practice it, mindfulness allows you to focus on what is happening to *you* in the present moment.

When you practice mindfulness, you practice authenticity, openness, intentionality, and grace. Be authentically you. Live from your heart and your soul. Do not allow your ego or societal standards to control you. Be open. Openness is embracing yourself and what is around you. Seek the truth and learn from everything around you. Allow your environment to teach you. Do everything that you do with intention. Intentionally be kind. Be responsive and proactive, so not be reactive. Practice Grace. Accept what is around you. Allow grace to show you how to forgive and love what is imperfect for what it is.

Mindfulness is centered around Buddhism and comes from the practice of "sati." Buddha and his followers teach that it is important to live in the present moment. Mindfulness is bringing your attention to the "now" rather than focusing on what you cannot control. The Buddhist term "sati" is the understanding of the full range of yourself. Buddhism teaches "sati" as a constant repetition of being mindful and thoughtful. Mindfulness is a simple practice, but getting it right can be complex. Mindfulness comes with many benefits that will be discussed in further chapters. Mindfulness is not meant to be a "quick-fix" program. Instead, it is intended to be an adjustment of lifestyle: a change of attitude. When you are mindful, you are better. You can practice mindfulness to whatever extent you may wish. Obviously, the more you implement mindfulness into every part of your life, the more you will benefit from it. However, even if you are only able to utilize mindfulness in a few simple areas, you will still find some benefit from it. Being mindful will never be a bad thing for you. Others will never be mad at you for focusing more on your present moment. Mindfulness is a change for the better.

Chapter 3: Benefits of Mindfulness

"This is a wonderful day; I've never seen this one before." – Maya Angelou

Mindfulness comes with a host of benefits. Some of these will come from a simple and small application and understanding of mindfulness, and some benefits require additional work, focus, and dedication. Take on Mindfulness if you are ready to experience better for yourself. Give yourself the life of focus and present-living that you deserve.

- **Reduce Stress:** Do you find yourself constantly overwhelmed by stress? Practicing mindfulness has been proven to be successful as a helpful tool. Take a step back and appreciate what is around you. Having stress levels that are too high for you can have disastrous consequences. Studies show that those who are more stressed have shorter lives, are unhappy, have worse health problems, and have people around them who are unhappy. Practicing mindfulness can make a huge difference in your stress levels and your life. That alone should be reason to give it a shot.

- **Improve Health:** Helping your health is always vitally important. Those who slow down and take an extra look around tend to be healthier and happier. Who wouldn't want to add years to their own life-time. Not just bad years, but years in which you can truly appreciate what is right in front of you and how you are swimming through life. Focusing on the present is a fantastic way to improve your future. You may not even realize this just yet.

Do you have trouble losing weight? Are you constantly in pain? Do you have health issues that you just cannot get under control? Improving your health through mindfulness can make everything better. Don't waste time worrying and making your own personal health worse, take some time to enjoy your life as it passes by and you become healthier. Mindfulness has been proven to make your own health better. Just think about it!

- **Increase Focus:** Do you have trouble staying focus? You are trying to get something done and you keep switching over to the Facebook tab on your computer to see what your friends are up to? Do you find yourself looking at your phone more than you are looking at the people who are around you? It sounds like you may have some focus issues. Mindfulness is the act of intentionally focusing. Focus is a muscle that you have to consistently use and strengthen. The more you allow your mind to wander, the more it will wander. Utilize mindfulness to set a strong example for your subconscious. Using mindfulness can increase your focus and make difficult tasks seem a million times easier. That's not something you want to take for granted. Using your own mindfulness capabilities can only improve your focus and make your life and daily tasks easier. Those around you will soon be impressed and happy with your improved focus. They will want to learn your secret. You can help improve the focus of everyone you spend time with as well: simply share mindfulness with them.

- **Reduce Anxiety:** Worry, stress, anxiety: none of this is good for you or those around you. Anxiety can be crippling and far from fun and helpful. Anxiety can keep you from getting out of bed in the morning or taking on big tasks. Anxiety can severely hurt your social relationships. Anxiety is a monster that you do not want to feed. Practicing mindfulness has been known to improve anxiety. It teaches you focus on what is the present. Stop worrying about the way that someone talked to you or the way that work is going to go tomorrow. Focus on the present and put away the past. Anxiety makes this very difficult and mindfulness can help with this. Mindfulness has been known to improve anxiety issues. However, if you do not have anxiety issues, mindfulness may help you out through other parts of your life and solve other issues. Do not count mindfulness as an option out even if anxiety is not as issue that you need to worry about.

- **Increase Happiness:** Who doesn't want to be happier? Happiness can be hard to accomplish if you are not focused on the present. Instead, you are focused on the past and worried about what could have happened. If you are focused on the future and what might happen, you cannot enjoy the present. Mindfulness can make you happier by encouraging you to live in the present moment. Appreciate the time that you have and the useful moments that you have. Happiness can be found by those who are mindful.

- **Better Social Relationships:** Do you want to be the friend that truly enjoys themselves in every social situation and everyone loves being around? There is always a friend who notices when people get haircuts and when people are upset. These types of skills come with improved focus and concentration. Mindfulness can help you accomplish this. Having stronger social skills can improve many things about your life and business adventures. Mindfulness can help improve your social relationships. In turn, this can make those people in your family and friend circles happier and more impressed by you. Do not underestimate the power of a strong friend and happy family. Do not underestimate the strong impact that mindfulness can have on your life.

- **Reduce Depression:** Sadness and depression can run your life ragged. Many people have found mindfulness to be useful in the treatment and reduction of depression. When you practice mindfulness, you can take in those things that negetivly effect you and adjust your environment. Stopping and slowing down can give you the opportunity to identify your triggers to both deep depression and happiness. It can help you identify what areas you are happiest in and keep you there. Mindfulness is not the one-stop-depression solution. It can take additional work and dedication.

Remember if you have thoughts of suicide or hurting others you need to seek help immediately. Mindfulness cannot solve these things on its own. Mindfulness combined with proper treatment, help, and support may make all the difference in the world. It may help you reduce or eliminate your depression.

- **New Experiences:** Mindfulness can open you up to trying and taking advantage of new experiences. It can assist you in conquering your feelings of fear. Try that skydiving adventure! This is what mindfulness can help you with. Keep yourself strong and adventurous. Mindfulness can encourage you to try new things and see new parts of your own existence. You may find that there is a brand new beautiful part of your own life that you haven't seen before. Mindfulness encourages you to take advantage of these new experiences and appreciate them. Notice when a new opportunity presents itself and gives you the opportunity to appreciate something else. This improvement on your life will make a larger difference than you realize. Perhaps one of the more enlightening things about mindfulness is the enlightenment itself. It allows you to see what you did not see before and enjoy new experiences that you may not have enjoyed before.

- **Increased Openness:** Very similar to your amount of new experiences will be your increased openness. Your willingness to see and be open to new, unexpected chapters in your life will give you the best opportunity to take advantage of mindfulness.

- **Greater Appreciation:** Not only will you be open to these new experiences and sights, but mindfulness lets you appreciate that. There is power in appreciation. Learning to appreciate the things you see in everyday life will give you the ability to be happy with where you are. Appreciating the people around you will give you the ability to improve your own social relationships. Learn as much as you can from the moment you are in.

- **Weight Loss:** Mindfulness can help you lose weight! Did you know that there is a way to improve your own dieting and ambitious goals for your own personal health? Mindfulness makes it easier! When you are mindful about what you eat you pay attention to every single bit that you take. When you pay this much attention and give this much focus to what is going on in the present, it makes it easier to make good decisions. Mindfulness, and mindful eating can make a huge difference in your life and your own weight loss.

- **Better Decisions:** Mindfulness encourages you to make better and stronger decisions for your own life. It tells you to focus on what it is important. When you make decisions, mindfulness teaches you to take the time to make the right one. In the same respect, it gives you the framework to teach yourself how to make these decisions without extreme fear. You can make these decisions without fear of what the past has done to you and without fear of what the future may hold. Instead, you make the right decision for yourself.

- **Emotional Intelligence:** Emotional intelligence is an important part of living your everyday life. You must have the intelligence to identify and work with your own emotions and the emotions of other. Having strong emotional intelligence will make you feel better and make those around you more comfortable. Practicing mindfulness gives you the opportunity to have a good amount of emotional intelligence. This is an important personal asset that will only benefit you as a member of society. Think about the people you prefer to spend your time with, are they emotionally intelligent? Why? Do they make you feel comfortable and calm when you are around them? This is a very valued skill which you should practice. Utilize mindfulness to increase your own emotional intelligence.

- **Peace:** Do you want to be calm? Mindfulness can bring you an inner peace that you did not know was possible. It is important that you feel peace and emulate this to those around you. Peacefulness can make a big difference in your life. If you are searching for peace, give mindfulness a try: you will be glad you did.

Chapter 4: Where to Start

"The mind is just like a muscle - the more you exercise it, the stronger it gets and the more it can expand." - Idowu Koyenikan

So you have examined the benefits of mindfulness and you are ready to begin. Where do you start? How do you begin to enlighten yourself and push yourself to a higher plane of mindfulness? Here's where we suggest you begin.

Take a minute to examine where you are sitting. Answer these questions about your current environment:

- Where are you sitting?

- How do you feel about your current environment?
- What colors, feelings, and sights are directly in front of and around you?
- What is your body feeling?
- Focus on the way your body feels against the surface you are sitting on.
- Do you feel cold or warm?
- How do your clothes feel on your skin?

The first important step in practicing mindfulness is examining your environment. Slow down, and take stock of yourself and where you are. Take the time to center yourself in your environment.

These are tactics that you are going to want to utilize daily. If you feel yourself getting overwhelmed, stop and center yourself in your environment. Ask yourself some questions and calm down by focusing on what is directly in front of you. Work to pull your focus away from those events of the past or worries of the future. Instead, find yourself a strong moment of peace in which you can temporarily dwell. These moments are going to be easier to find if you start practicing simple mindfulness meditation each day. This small technique will leave you learning. You can do it as much or as little as you may choose. That is the fun part of mindfulness: it is what you make it.

Mindfulness meditation is where you will want to begin. Having a good mindfulness meditation session is going to make your entire day easier. Start slow. Set aside ten minutes of your day to practice a good, mindfulness meditation. This will give you the chance to re-center and feel better about yourself.

Basic Mindfulness Meditation: Find a comfortable place to sit quietly without distraction or too much noise. If you have a hard time blocking out noise, utilize headphones and calming meditation music. Spend several minutes focusing on your breathing and repeating a word or mantra to yourself. Utilize mindfulness quotes if need be. Allow your thoughts to pass without judgement. Acknowledge them, but do not dwell on them.

Notice subtle changes and sensations in your body such as itches. Allow them to pass without judgement or concern. It is simply there, do not allow it to affect you.

Notice what is around you. Notice the sights, sounds, and smells. Acknowledge them, then allow them to pass without judgement. Do not allow them to crowd your thoughts.

How do you feel? Consider your emotions. Anger, fear, sadness: allow them to pass without judgement. These are emotions you cannot control. Acknowledge that they are there and move on. Continue to focus on your breathing and repeating your word or mantra (your word or mantra does not have to be repeated out loud, this is totally up to you).

Cravings and urges can attack you as you are attempting to meditate. Take that urge or craving and let it pass without judgement. Replace the wish you have for the craving to go away with the certain knowledge that it will. Continue your focus.

Chapter 5: Practicing Your Mindfulness

"Life is a dance. Mindfulness is witnessing that dance." -Amit Ray

Go with the Flow

It is important that you go with the flow of life. Recognize that life follows a natural pattern and flow. There is natural pattern and ebb that your life will follow. If you recognize that life is not going to follow a constant high, you will be able to be happier and calmer. Go with the flow as much as possible. This is an important tenant of mindfulness. Observe the flow of nature around you. Observe your own flow. Observe the flow of your body, emotions, cravings, and thoughts. Allow them to pass without judgement and difficulty. Do not let your flow affect your peace and ability. Let the flow of life pass without concern or judgement. Replace worries with the knowledge that life will continue to go on without judgement.

Pay Attention

As you take on mindfulness and meditation, you will notice external sensations like sounds, sights, and touch that make up your moment-to-moment experience. The challenge is not to latch onto a particular idea, emotion, or sensation, or to get caught in thinking about the past or the future. Instead you should watch what comes and goes in your mind, and discover which mental habits produce a feeling of well-being or suffering.

Stay with It

This process may not seem relaxing or helpful to you at all. Mindfulness does not come with immediate results. It takes dedication and lots of work to get to a point where you will notice success. However, mindfulness will create these positive results for you as long as you stick with it. Work hard to practice meditation and letting thoughts pass through without judgement. Stay with mindfulness! It will help you out!

Practice Acceptance

There is a reason that the motto of Alcoholics Anonymous includes the concept of "to accept the things I cannot change." This is something that you want to focus on and practice each day. Accept your environment. Accept the people around you. Accept the feelings that you have. Accept your cravings. Accept that everything is temporary. Practice acceptance. This can be vital to your success in mindfulness.

Gently Redirect

Your mind will wander. Thoughts and feelings will cross your mind. Things will try to de-rail you. The natural direction of life will feel as though it is not natural at all. Try to consistently and gently redirect yourself to mindfulness. Know that you have the ability to let everything pass without judgement. Gently redirecting your life can be difficult. Even this can feel as though it is not helping you at all. Take your time as you practice your mindfulness.

Cultivate Mindfulness Moment to Moment

Mindfulness is not just about formal meditation; you can also cultivate mindfulness informally by focusing your attention on your moment-to-moment sensations during everyday activities. This is done by single-tasking—doing one thing at a time and giving it your full attention. As you floss your teeth, pet the dog, or eat an apple, slow down the process and be fully present as it unfolds and involves all of your senses. As you complete these tasks, it is okay to have other thoughts and worries. However, just as if you are meditating take a moment to allow the thoughts and worries to pass without judgement. Let your fears pass with knowledge that they will subside.

Develop a Daily Practice

It is important that you develop a daily practice of mindfulness. Get in the habit of completing a good mindful meditation. This may be multiple times a day or just once a day. Either way, sticking to a daily practice and daily plan will help you succeed in your goal to become more mindful. Practice your mindfulness thoughtfully. Meditate at the times during the day that will be the most successful for you. Here are six good steps to follow when you create a daily practice and routine:

1. Find a suitable place to meditate. Make sure that this is somewhere where you feel comfortable and safe.

2. Select a regular time to practice. Make sure that this time is one that will work well for you on any day.

3. Find a posture that works for you. This posture should be comfortable and not strain you.

4. Bring your attention to your breath. Allow yourself to feel the sensations of your breathing.

5. Allow your mind to wander, but take the time to re-focus it.

6. Let your breathing become natural.

Chapter 6: Meditations

"Be happy in the moment, that's enough. Each moment is all we need, not more."-Mother Teresa

Chocolate Meditation: Many Buddhist and meditation traditions use nuts or berries to meditate. You can utilize chocolate. Find a comfortable place to sit. Pick out your favorite chocolate. Give yourself several minutes of alone, undisturbed time. Begin by looking at the wrapper of your chocolate. Appreciate where it came from and how it got to you. Appreciate that the wrapper is intended to keep your chocolate bar safe. Consider how the colors of the wrapper make you feel and how they entice you to eat it. Think about how the texture of the wrapper makes you feel. How does it sit on the bar? Next, open it slowly. Appreciate how it opens. Think about how the opening of the bar makes you feel. Smell the chocolate. Does it bring back memories? Does it make you happy? What flavors can you get just from the scent? Take a small taste. Appreciate how the chocolate feels on your tongue. Think about the different flavors. Move the chocolate around your mouth and allow it to melt. Take advantage of every ounce of flavor from that bite before you move onto the next one. Take a moment to recall the bite you just took. Take the next bite, and repeat.

Body Evaluation: The meditation gives you a moment to take stock of your body and how you are feeling. Find a comfortable place to sit or lay. Find a comfortable rhythm of breathing. Turn on calming music if you wish. Take turns flexing and relaxing your muscles. Internally consider each inch on your body. Doing this may cause you to fall asleep. If you need to, turn on an alarm. Think about everything that your toes have done for you. Appreciate and consider them. How do they feel? How do you feel about them? Move onto you right foot, then your left. Continue like this to every part of your body. This meditation gives you a second to re-center and re-connect with your body and how it is feeling. It also allows you to appreciate your body and everything it accomplishes. It is so easy for us to put ourselves down that we lose sight of how great we really are. When you do this meditation, think about just how brilliant your body is. Think about how much it does for you and how proud you are of it. The human body is fantastic, the includes yours too.

Repeat: This is the mediation that is discussed earlier in the book.

Find a comfortable place to sit quietly without distraction or too much noise. If you have a hard time blocking out noise, utilize headphones and calming meditation music. Spend several minutes focusing on your breathing and repeating a word or mantra to yourself. Utilize mindfulness quotes if need be. Allow your thoughts to pass without judgement. Acknowledge them, but do not dwell on them.

Notice subtle changes and sensations in your body such as itches. Allow them to pass without judgement or concern. It is simply there, do not allow it to affect you.

Notice what is around you. Notice the sights, sounds, and smells. Acknowledge them, then allow them to pass without judgement. Do not allow them to crowd your thoughts.

How do you feel? Consider your emotions. Anger, fear, sadness: allow them to pass without judgement. These are emotions you cannot control. Acknowledge that they are there and move on. Continue to focus on your breathing and repeating your word or mantra (your word or mantra does not have to be repeated out loud, this is totally up to you).

Cravings and urges can attack you as you are attempting to meditate. Take that urge or craving and let it pass without judgement. Replace the wish you have for the craving to go away with the certain knowledge that it will. Continue your focus.

Utilize these meditations to give yourself a good advantage. There are others available. You can use websites like YouTube to find guided mediations. Find mantras, words, and quotes that work for you. Mindfulness is really what you make of it. Sit back, and appreciate what is right in front of you. Appreciate what you have. Do not become overwhelmed with worry of the future. Know that what will come, will come. Worrying about it changes nothing. Do not become consumed with mistakes or faults of the past. These have happened and you cannot change them. Allow mindfulness to be your own practice of utilizing your mind. Utilizing your ability to analyze and comprehend: examine those areas and ideas that you would not normally examine.

Chapter 7: Dos and Do Nots

"We have only now, only this single eternal moment opening and unfolding before us, day and night." -
Jack Kornfield

Do

- Do stay calm.

- Consistently re-center yourself.

- Meditate. These can be structured, guided, general ideas, or just playing sitting calmly.

- Share with others. Allow your friends and family to share and help you along your way. Let them see how mindfulness helps you and can help others.

- Follow the teachings of Buddha. Mindfulness is rooted in Buddha. Examine his teachings as guidelines and standards for working on mindfulness. Buddha and Buddhist teachers all have fantastic teachings that can help you along your journey to mindfulness.

- Focus on what is in front of you.

- Create a daily routine. This routine should include plenty of time to practice mindfulness.

- Be aware of what you are doing and where you are at all times.

- Practice mindful eating.

- Practice mindful exercising.

- Continue to do research. You are not the only one out there who is hoping to practice mindfulness. Utilize this as a helping hand as you practice mindfulness. They may come up with new meditations and mantras to help you along.

- Find your favorite mantras. Examine the quotes in this book along with your own life. Find a mantra that will make you feel better and keep you centered and focused as you work through your every day life.
- Practice meditation when you feel overwhelmed and unfocused.
- Call others for help.
- Call for help if you have thoughts of suicide or hurting others.
- Do remember that feelings are temporary.
- Do remember that you are allowed to have feelings
- Do allow your feelings and thoughts to pass without judgement or fear.

Do not

- Do not freak out.
- Do not stress about the past.

- Do not allow yourself to become overwhelmed.

- Do not worry about what the future might bring.

- Do not judge your thoughts.

- Do not judge your feelings.

- Do not judge others.

- Do not judge your environment.

- Do not worry about everything around you.

Utilize the do's and do not's to help you work through your struggles and mindfulness. Give yourself the best chance possible to succeed. Add your own items to the lists as you learn what is effective for you and what is not. As you study Buddha and other mindfulness teachers, you can learn more and more about yourself. Make your own lists and keep your own reminders about what to do and what not to do.

That is going to be the best way to grow and mature in your own mindfulness adventure.

Chapter 8: Mindful Eating

"The more you eat, the less flavor; the less you eat, the more flavor." -Chinese Proverb

Mindful eating a great way to practice mindfulness. If you can make sure that you are eating mindfully, you can practice mindfulness with every meal. This adjustment to your eating will make a huge difference in your life. Practicing mindfulness while you eat can increase your chances of losing weight and being healthier. Do you want to lose weight and be more conscious of the way that you are eating? Try your hand and mindful eating today. Mindful eating is a great way to enjoy your food more. It encourages you to focus and savor it. You will remember how things taste and how you like them. If you are mindful about the way that you eat, you can begin to crush cravings and other issues. Mindfulness encourages you to acknowledge cravings without judgement and with the understanding that they will subside. You may crave cake now, but mindfulness encourages you to know that if you do not get that cake, your craving will subside. You will be no worse for the wear. Here are some important steps to mindful eating:

1. **Edit your shopping List.** Consider the healthiness of every item you add to your list and stick to it. This will help you to avoid impulse buys when you are shopping. Fill most of your cart in the produce section and avoid the center aisles. Center isles are filled with processed foods. Avoid the chips and candy at the check-out counter.

2. **Gauge your Hunger.** Come to the table with an appetite, not when you are ravenously hungry. If you skip meals, you may be eager to get anything in your stomach and your first priority will be filling it up rather than eating the food that you should be eating. It is important that you don't wait hours and hours between eating. Be mindful of when your stomach tells you that it is time to eat. Listen to it, not your cravings.

3. **Portion Size!** Start with a small portion. Eat only until you are full.

4. **Appreciate your food.** Pause for a minute or two before you begin eating to contemplate everything and everyone it took to bring the meal to your table. Silently express your thanks for the

opportunity to enjoy delicious food and the people you are eating and enjoying it with.

5. **Senses.** Bring all your senses to your eating. When you are cooking, serving, and eating your food, be attentive to color, texture, aroma, and even the sounds different foods make as you prepare them. As you chew your food, try to notice or find all of the ingredients, especially seasonings.

6. **Take small bites.** It's easier to taste food completely when your mouth isn't full. Put down your utensil between bites.

7. **Chew thoroughly.** Chew each bite well until you can taste the essence and all of the flavors of the food. (You may have to chew each mouthful 20 to

40 times, depending on the food.) You may be surprised at all the flavors that are released.

8. **Eat slowly.** If you follow the advice above, you won't chow down on your food and finish it feeling unhappy and ungrateful. Devote at least five minutes to mindful eating before you chat with your tablemates.

Utilizing these mindful steps can bring a whole new light to the way that you are eating. You will get to enjoy to food you are eating more. It will be easier for your body to tell you when you are full and when you should stop eating. You may find that this type of eating makes you feel stronger and enjoy spending time around the table more. Mindful eating gives you the opportunity to control your impulses and avoid over-eating. Not only that, but if you are appreciating the way that food tastes more as you are eating it, you will not have cravings for processed foods, but instead have cravings for foods which give you the ability to enjoy them more.

Chapter 9: Starting and Ending Your Day Right

"Mindful and creative, a child who has neither a past, nor examples to follow, nor value judgments, simply lives, speaks and plays in freedom." - *Arnaud Desjardins*

When you get out of bed in the morning, allow yourself to immediately start your day off right. Before even standing up, take a moment to consider where you are. Appreciate the fact that you are in a warm house with a roof over your head. Appreciate the covers you have to keep you warm and comfortable at night. Appreciate the fact that you are awake right now. Appreciate those around you. Take a moment to consider every part of your body and how it feels. Consider from the tips of the toes to your hair. Stretch and appreciate the muscles that you have. Before you worry about what is coming next in your day, consider yourself. Decide on a mantra and begin repeating it. Start your day off on a positive note. This should help you out considerably.

In the same respect, you want to make sure that you are ending your day right. Take time to decompress from the stress of the day. Let go what happened during the day and give yourself some time to relax. Allow yourself to be happy with where you are. This would be a good time to consider doing a meditation.

Chapter 10: Quotes to Help

Use these quotes to give yourself an extra boost as you take on your new mindfulness challenge. Mindfulness can change your life if you allow it to. Mindfulness is what you make of it. Good luck on your journey.

"When you realize nothing is lacking, the whole world belongs to you." -Lao Tzu

"Drink your tea slowly and reverently, as if it is the axis on which the world earth revolves – slowly, evenly, without rushing toward the future; live the actual moment. Only this moment is life." -Thich Nhat Hanh"

"As soon as we wish to be happier, we are no longer happy." -Walter Landor

"The best way to capture moments is to pay attention. This is how we cultivate mindfulness. Mindfulness means being awake. It means knowing what you are doing." -Jon Kabat-Zinn

"In today's rush, we all think too much — seek too much — want too much — and forget about the joy of just being." -Eckhart Tolle

"If you want others to be happy, practice compassion. If you want to be happy, practice compassion." -Dalai Lama

"Suffering usually relates to wanting things to be different than they are." -Allan Lokos

"If we learn to open our hearts, anyone, including the people who drive us crazy, can be our teacher." -Pema Chodron

"If the doors of perception were cleansed, everything would appear to man as it is, infinite." -William Blake

"Feelings come and go like clouds in a windy sky. Conscious breathing is my anchor." - Thich Nhat Hanh

"If you want to conquer the anxiety of life, live in the moment, live in the breath." -Amit Ray

"To diminish the suffering of pain, we need to make a crucial distinction between the pain of pain, and the pain we create by our thoughts about the pain. Fear, anger, guilt, loneliness and helplessness are all mental and emotional responses that can intensify pain." -Howard Cutler

"In the end, just three things matter: How well we have lived. How well we have loved. How well we have learned to let go" -Jack Kornfield

"Do every act of your life as though it were the last act of your life." -Marcus Aurelius

"Everything is created twice, first in the mind and then in reality." -Robin S. Sharma

"Don't believe everything you think. Thoughts are just that – thoughts." -Allan Lokos

"Respond; don't react. Listen; don't talk. Think; don't assume." -Raji Lukkoor

"In this moment, there is plenty of time. In this moment, you are precisely as you should be. In this moment, there is infinite possibility." -Victoria Moran

"Mindfulness is simply being aware of what is happening right now without wishing it were different; enjoying the pleasant without holding on when it changes (which it will);

being with the unpleasant without fearing it will always be this way (which it won't)." - James Baraz

"Mindfulness isn't difficult; we just need to remember to do it." -Sharon Salzberg

"It's only when we truly know and understand that we have a limited time on earth – and that we have no way of knowing when our time is up – that we will begin to live each day to the fullest, as if it was the only one we had." – Elisabeth Kübler-Ross

"Begin at once to live, and count each separate day as a separate life." -Seneca

"The way to live in the present is to remember that 'This too shall pass.' When you experience joy, remembering that 'This too shall pass' helps you savor the here and now. When you experience pain and sorrow, remembering that 'This too shall pass' reminds you that grief, like joy, is only temporary."
-Joey Green

"If you concentrate on finding whatever is good in every situation, you will discover that your life will suddenly be filled with gratitude, a feeling that nurtures the soul."

-Rabbi Harold Kushner

"There's only one reason why you're not experiencing bliss at this present moment, and it's because you're thinking or focusing on what you don't have.... But, right now you have everything you need to be in bliss."
-Anthony de Mello

"We are awakened to the profound realization that the true path to liberation is to let go of everything."
-Jack Kornfield

Made in the USA
Lexington, KY
08 May 2017